YOU CAN STAY IN CONTROL: WILD OR CALM?

You Choose the Ending

Do you ever wish you could change a story or choose a different ending?

IN THESE BOOKS, YOU CAN!

Read along and when you see this:

WHAT HAPPENS NEXT?

Skip to the page for that choice, and see what happens.

What happens when Toby's mom brings home a new baby? Will Toby be wild or calm? Help Toby make choices by reading this book.

Toby is excited. Baby Max is finally here. Toby feels like he has been waiting forever to meet his new baby brother.

WHAT HAPPENS NEXT?

→ If Toby jumps around wildly when his mom comes in, turn the page.
If Toby stays calm, turn to page 20. ←

Toby jumps up and down. He's so excited,
he just can't stop. "Be careful, Toby!" Mom says.
"Max is very little. We need to be calm around him."

TURN THE PAGE →

"Let me see Max!" Toby says. He tries to grab the baby. "Toby!" his mother warns. "You are being too wild. Sit down and I will let you see your new brother."

WHAT HAPPENS NEXT?

→ If Toby keeps grabbing for Max, turn the page.
If Toby sits on the couch, turn to page 18. ←

Toby wants to touch his brother. He doesn't wait. Instead, he grabs his brother's arms. He startles Max, and Max begins to cry. The loud crying surprises Toby. "Toby!" his mother cries.

WHAT HAPPENS NEXT?

→ If Toby reacts wildly to the noise, turn the page.
If Toby stays in control, turn to page 14. ←

Toby drops his brother's arms. He covers
his ears to block out Max's crying. He spins
in wild circles and begins to scream. He
tries to drown out his new brother's crying.

TURN THE PAGE →

Toby's mom puts her hand on her son's shoulder. "Toby, you need to be calm around Max. Your wild behavior could scare or hurt him. Please take a time out."

Toby stops. He sits down. Toby feels bad. He should have stayed calm. Now his mom is mad and he has to wait to hold Max.

THE END

↳ Go to page 23. ←

Toby stops. He hears Max crying. He sees his brother's fists curled tightly. Toby has upset Max. "I'm sorry," Toby says. "I was too wild."

TURN THE PAGE →

15

Toby calms his body down. He breathes slowly through his nose. He relaxes his muscles. Max's crying grows softer.

"It's okay, Toby," says his mother, "but we will need to wait for Max to calm down before you can hold him." Toby is disappointed, but now he knows that he needs to stay calm to hold his brother.

THE END

Go to page 23.

Toby listens to his mother's words. He puts his arms down. He goes to the couch and sits down next to Mom. Toby calmly strokes the baby's head.

"I'm proud of you for calming down, Toby," his mother says.

TURN TO PAGE 22 →

Toby feels wild inside. He wants to play with his brother.
But the baby is sleeping. So Toby controls his body.
"Can I hold my new brother, Mom?" Toby asks quietly.
"Of course," Mom replies.

TURN THE PAGE →

Toby's mother gently places the sleeping baby into Toby's arms. "I love you, Max," Toby says. Toby knows they will be best friends.

THE END

- What choices did you make for Toby? How did that story end?
- Read the story again and try different choices.
  How did the story change?
- How did Toby calm himself down?
  Could you do that to calm your body?
- When is it important to stay calm?
  When is it okay to be wild?

We are all free to make choices, but choices have consequences. What would YOU do if you were so excited you couldn't control yourself?

For Karina and the Rose Boys—C.C.M.

AMICUS ILLUSTRATED and AMICUS INK
are published by Amicus
P.O. Box 1329, Mankato, MN 56002
www.amicuspublishing.us

Library of Congress Cataloging-in-Publication Data
Names: Miller, Connie Colwell, 1976- author. | Assanelli, Victoria, 1984- illustrator.
Title: You can stay in control : wild or calm? / by Connie Colwell Miller ;
    illustrated by Victoria Assanelli.
Description: Mankato, Minnesota : Amicus, [2018] | Series: Making good choices
Identifiers: LCCN 2016057213 (print) | LCCN 2017009610 (ebook) |
    ISBN 9781681511658 (library binding) | ISBN 9781681512556 (ebook) |
    ISBN 9781681522340 (pbk.)
Subjects: LCSH: Calmness—Juvenile literature. | Agitation (Psychology—Juvenile
    literature. | Decision making in children—Juvenile literature.
Classification: LCC BF575.C35 M55 2018 (print) | LCC BF575.C35 (ebook) |
    DDC 155.4/19—dc23
LC record available at https://lccn.loc.gov/2016057213

Editor: Rebecca Glaser
Designer: Kathleen Petelinsek

Printed in China
HC 10 9 8 7 6 5 4 3 2 1
PB 10 9 8 7 6 5 4 3 2 1

ABOUT THE AUTHOR

Connie Colwell Miller is a writer, editor, and instructor who lives in Mankato, Minnesota, with her four children. She has written over 80 books for young children. She likes to tell stories to her kids to teach them important life lessons.

ABOUT THE ILLUSTRATOR

Victoria Assanelli was born during the autumn of 1984 in Buenos Aires, Argentina. She spent most of her childhood playing with her grandparents, reading books, and drawing doodles. She began working as an illustrator in 2007, and has illustrated several textbooks and storybooks since.